# KITTENS

## A PORTRAIT OF THE ANIMAL WORLD

**Marcus Schneck**

# TODTRI

This book was designed and produced by
Todtri Productions Limited
P.O. Box 20058
New York, NY 10023-1482
Fax: (212) 279-1241

Printed and bound in Singapore

ISBN 1-880908-30-1


*Author:* Marcus Schneck

*Producer:* Robert M. Tod
*Book Designer:* Mark Weinberg
*Photo editor:* Edward Douglas
*Editors:* Don Kennison, Shawna Kimber
*Production Co-ordinator:* Heather Weigel
*DTP Associate:* Jackie Skyroczky
*Typesetting:* Command-O, NYC

*Printed and bound in Singapore by Tien Wah Press*

## PHOTO CREDITS

**Photographer**/Page Number

**Dembinsky Photo Associates**
Larime Photographic 6, 10, 13, 17(top), 26, 36 (bottom), 70, 74

**Dorothy Holby** 11 (top), 12 (bottom), 14 (top), 20 (top & bottom),
21, 24-25, 30 (bottom), 33, 36 (top), 46 (top), 49 (bottom), 64, 65,
66, 67, 69 (top), 71, 72-73, 75 (top), 78

**Ron Kimball** 3, 4, 5, 8-9, 12 (top), 14 (bottom), 15 (bottom),
16, 17 (bottom), 18, 23, 27, 28 (top & bottom), 31 (top & bottom),
32 (top & bottom), 34, 38, 39, 40-41, 42, 44, 45, 46 (bottom), 49 (top),
50, 51, 52 (top & bottom), 53, 55, 56-57, 58, 59, 60, 61, 62,
63, 68 (top), 75 (bottom), 76, 77 (top & bottom), 79

**Sally Klein** 7, 19, 35, 37, 47, 54, 68 (bottom), 69 (bottom)

**Pets by Paulette** 11 (bottom), 15 (top), 22, 30 (top), 48

**Picture Perfect, USA**
Bruno Zarri 43

**Tom Stack & Associates**
Barbara Von Hoffman 29

# INTRODUCTION

*Every object, whether living or inanimate, is cause for new exploration by the kitten. Initial contact usually is tentative and probing, allowing plenty of possibility for escape.*

F ew of us can resist the allure that a kitten brings—its tiny, wide-eyed, cuddly presence is something we all respond to. In part we're reacting to a long-standing human emotion toward small, seemingly helpless creatures. Our affection for kittens extends back millennia to our ancient forebears.

The earliest recorded linkage between man and cat dates back to Egypt in 3000 B.C. African wild cats (**Felis libyca**) were naturally drawn to the huge populations of rats, mice, and other vermin that infested the grain stores of the Egyptians. In turn the keepers of those stores came to recognise the cats' abilities in rodent-control. They encouraged these wild cats to take up residence within and around their granaries.

At first this was a separate though complementary relationship. The cats kept their distance from the humans and spent most of their time in the shadows, quietly going about their task as mousers. Gradually, however, exposure to humans wore down the cats' comfortable distance and direct physical encounters began to occur.

Adult wild cats would bring their kitten litters on their hunting forays into the grain storage areas, and the instinctive barriers to human contact were further broken down in subsequent generations of the animals. Soon enough, the cats were living much of their lives within the confines of the granaries, and also giving birth to their kittens in these new shelters.

Impressed with their rodent-destroying capabilities as well as their physical attributes, the Egyptians came to view cats as something sacred. And as the numbers of cats in the human cities grew, people were willing to take them into their homes.

Similar scenarios occurred in other parts of the world, although at significantly later times—notably with the European wild cat (F. silvestris), the desert cat of Asia (F. ornata), and the longhair (F. manul) of central Asia.

No written records reveal how well the special attribute of kitten cuteness played in the development of the human-cat relationship, but there can be no doubt that it was a significant factor in helping humans to decide that this animal—above so many others—should come to share their living space and their lives.

The completely content kitten, and adult cat for that matter, often will be heard purring in the pleasure it takes in such a comfortable state.

Exploration gradually becomes a bigger and bigger part of the kitten's life, as it reaches out beyond the nest and the litter to begin claiming its own piece of the world.

# BEGINNING OF LIFE

A kitten comes into this world with only its mother to care for it. The bond between a mother and father cat is weak at best when the female is in heat and generally nonexistent after the mating has taken place. The male has long since disappeared by the time kittens arrive.

Sometimes another female, familiar to and accepted by the queen, will assist with the birthing in something akin to a midwife role. However, after the kittens are born, it is once again entirely up to the mother for their care.

In general, queens are very good mothers. Natural selection favours the offspring of individuals with the best mothering skills. The young will be better fed and guarded, and will receive good lessons in the strategies necessary for survival as adults.

## Birth

Generally kittens are born in a nest of their mother's choosing. This often is a dark, warm, quiet spot that is hidden and easily defended. However, some queens who feel a great deal of safety and comfort with their surroundings, such as in a familiar home, will simply choose a favoured spot, which just may be their regular bed. But the location usually will be the result of some consideration by the queen, who may even spend several days making the choice. Once she has, the queen will remain close to the nest, withdrawing into it as soon as she feels the onset of labor.

Each kitten, upon emerging from the birth canal, receives a licking by the queen, which not only removes birthing juices but also helps stimulate breathing in the newborn. The queen will next bite through the umbilical cord and eat the afterbirth. (This action is a remnant from the cat's wild ancestry, when removal of such enemy-attracting smells was an absolute necessity.) After all this has been accomplished with the entire litter, the

*Following page: The world beyond their nest is a big, strange, and confusing place to these Maine coon kittens, but it also holds a fascination that will draw them more and more away from the nest and out on their own.*

*Within their first few days kittens establish favourite feeding stations at their mother's teats, with the area around that individual nipple soon acquiring a special smell for them.*

*Kittens are born predators. The hunting instinct is a basic component of their very being, which includes actions such as stalking and ambush.*

7

mother will spend some time cleaning herself. She will then curl her body in a warm, protective curve around her kittens, and encourage them to begin nursing by directing them toward her teats, gently pushing and licking them.

## First Days

Kittens are born both blind and deaf. However, their sense of smell is strong at birth. This is critical for the nearly helpless babies in finding their way to their mother's teats to feed. They will respond to foreign smells right away, usually by spitting.

There is a good deal of struggling and pushing as the kittens first make the connection with the queen's teats. But before long, each of the kittens has decided upon a favorite teat. The area around that nipple soon takes on the particular scent of the specific kitten.

For the first day or two of its life, a kitten consumes colostrum from its mother's first milk. This substance gives the newborn protective antibodies necessary in seeing it through its initial six to ten weeks of life as it develops its own immunity.

The kittens also rely on their strong sense of smell to stay within the boundaries of the nest, or to find their way back if for any reason they have gone outside the nest. To such a sensitive little nose, their own nest smells completely different from any other place they might happen upon.

*For the first several weeks of their lives, kittens, like these three-week-old Persians, are nearly unable to provide for any of their own needs.*

*All kittens are born with their ears folded down and, hence, are temporarily deaf. For most breeds, however, the ears soon push into their normal erect position. The Scottish fold, at right, is an exception.*

*Plants are very attractive to kittens for many reasons. Unfortunately, many of our house plants also are dangerously poisonous to cats.*

Gradually the kitten begins to take more of an interest in the world beyond its nest, although its mother will remain a central figure for many more weeks.

Few creatures portray the image of complete helplessness and innocence as does a young kitten. What mischief could this adorable white Persian ever get into?

Many of the rules that govern cats in the wild, as well as their kittens, are subverted by the tender, nurturing assistance that owners generally give them in the home.

'Should we be doing this'? these two young Tonkinese kittens seem to be wondering. They may have been up for this new adventure when they climbed into the basket, but now second thoughts seem to have taken hold.

Kittens have good memories for things they see that relate directly to their lives and their comfort. They can be taught desired behaviour if the 'teacher' remembers this single critical point.

*The offspring of queens with good mothering skills are favoured by the process of natural selection because they receive a strong start to their lives.*

*The sense of smell is strong in kittens from their first day of life. It is the primary means by which they identify and find their mother, and by which she locates them.*

## A Mother's Touch

During at least the next couple of days, the queen will remain in almost constant contact with her litter. She may leave the nest to stretch, use the litter pan, eat, or drink, but will invariably return to the kittens within minutes.

Her normal sleep patterns will be greatly interrupted, both in duration and in depth. The newborns must nurse no less frequently than every two hours, and then the queen must lick each of their tummies to stimulate digestion and excretion. The mother also instinctively licks up and eats their excretions.

## Cat Senses

Cat eyes are much more effective than our own in dim light because the lens, cornea, and pupil are larger; because the feline eye is equipped with the tapetum lucidum, which is an area of reflective cells behind the retina; and because the retina contains more rods, which are the cells that provide for night vision.

The cat's ability to 'always' land on its feet is legendary to the point that many believe the animal to have a special sense in just this area. Actually this ability is a function of messages sent to the cat's brain by both its

eyes and a vestibular organ in its inner ear, which gauges the position of the head through a series of liquid, crystals, and tiny hairs.

The vestibular organ is fully developed in kittens from birth, but their eyes don't begin to open until, at the earliest, five days old and they may not fully open until twenty days. Thus during the period

*Kittens spend a great deal of their first few weeks of life asleep. Their bodies are undergoing growth and extreme changes, processes which require large expenditures of energy.*

*During the first weeks of their lives, kittens are almost constantly in contact with their mother, who leaves the nest only briefly for necessities such as eating, drinking, and using the litter pan.*

*Kittens very, very rarely come to know their fathers in any sort of parenting role. After mating with the queen, the tom generally disappears and returns to his bachelor lifestyle.*

from birth to when its eyes are opened fully, the kitten's 'righting' mechanism won't function properly.

## The Measure of Intelligence

One measure commonly applied to animal intelligence is the weight of the brain in relation to the length of the spinal cord. In other words, the comparison of brain size to body size. In this measure, cats rate a 4 to 1 ratio, whilst humans rate around 50 to 1.

From birth, the brain of the cat is that of a predator. The areas of the feline brain associated with the senses are extremely well developed. However, the area of the brain where intelligence is normally held—the frontal lobe—is relatively simple in comparison to some higher forms of life, such as apes and humans.

Some recent evidence suggests that certain breeds of cats are more intelligent than others. People defend their favourites by noting that some breeds only appear to be more intelligent because they have been bred for specific purposes.

Sometimes those who do not know cats very well attribute to them human characteristics, but most of the time what they perceive as intelligence is actually instinct, or what are known as feline rituals. Because a cat wants to lead a comfortable and satisfied life, it will learn certain routines out of what it perceives as a need to remain in the good graces of those around it. Thus what can seem a very intelligent cat may actually be one who assumes a role to retain or improve its status in its environment.

## The Ability to Learn

Cats most definitely do have the ability to learn. Using the litter pan, for example, is certainly a learnt behaviour, albeit one that coincides with a goal of the cat. There are those humans that are able to teach their feline charges 'tricks' similar to those taught to dogs. It is important to keep in mind whilst teaching cats that they don't respond to punishment.

Mounting evidence suggests that early learning in cats is essential to its properly performing tasks later in life—and the primary teacher is the queen. Mother cats appear to be amongst the best teachers in the animal kingdom. Kittens taken too early from their

*If this kitten should fall from the limb it more than likely will land on its feet due to quick reflexes; it responds to information supplied to its brain by both its eyes and a special vestibular organ located in the inner ear.*

*Tricks are not completely foreign to kittens, and even to adult cats. However, rather than learning something to please its owner, the kitten or cat may learn it for unknowable, internal reasons.*

*Licking is an essential part of being a cat. The queen licks the kittens clean immediately after birth and continues to clean them whilst they are under her care.*

*At about eight weeks of life kittens have their full set of milk teeth and, not coincidentally, by this point their mother generally has weaned them.*

mothers often demonstrate lessened abilities in some of the basic tasks of life, including use of litter pans.

## Mother as Teacher

Learning begins very early in a kitten's life. In addition to such basics as where food comes from and how to control all four of its legs at the same time, within just a few weeks the young cat is already adding to its knowledge about things like litter-box use.

And whilst cats do have memories, they are again filled only with those concepts needed to make their own lives more comfortable. Even for a kitten of only a few months in age,

remembering a name is not beyond the realm of possibility. Of course such response will come only if, in the cat's perspective, the name has been associated with good things. For example, use of the kitten's name when dinner is served is a good way for it to remember.

Anyone with a new kitten in the home will soon recognise other so-called tricks that the little cat has learnt. It will soon be calling the humans of the house to do its beckoning by, for instance, scratching or meowing. And it won't be long before it attempts to pry open the cabinet door where its treats are stored.

*Mother is everything to a young kitten. Not only does she supply all nourishment for the first several weeks of its life, she also is the sole line of defence and the primary teacher of skills the kitten will need later in life.*

## Becoming a Cat

Whilst the kitten is developing its repertoire of activities, its body is developing the tools it will need as an adult cat. For example, kittens' first teeth appear around the time their eyes open, and they generally have their full set of milk teeth by the age of eight weeks, which explains why this is usually the point at which their mothers have fully weaned them. A cat's permanent teeth appear between the ages of twelve and eighteen weeks, and despite the claims of some proponents of vegetarianism, these are the teeth of a carnivore.

As a matter of fact, cats are the most evolved family of carnivores. The feline digestive system is designed for using meat and eliminating its byproducts. To this end, the cat's intestines are relatively shorter than those of creatures with a more varied diet, such as humans and dogs. However, after generations of domestication and a diet not exclusively of meat, domestic cats have longer intestines in relation to the size of their bodies than do wild cats, such as lions and cougars.

The cat's need for vegetable matter in its diet remains. 'Greens' hold a constant attraction for our feline friends, and not just as food. Adult cats can be seen interacting with a variety household plants, and as soon as kittens begin to take solid foods regularly, they will begin to exhibit this same fascination. But at least for the first few weeks of life, nothing approaches mother's milk.

*Following page: Kittens usually are born in a nest that's been carefully selected by their mother for its seclusion and warmth. Queens who feel comfortable in the home often will use their regular bed as their nest.*

*Whilst many people would claim to see intelligence in the eyes of this kitten, more than likely this can be attributed to instinct.*

*'Stay, stay', pleaded the photographer whilst trying to get this shot, but most certainly whatever was dangled just out of this photo was what really persuaded the kitten to hold its pose.*

# DISCOVERING THE WORLD

The period between the time when the kitten begins to walk—approximately its third week of life—and the point when it makes the break from the litter—anywhere from three to six months—is critical to the kitten's normal and natural development into a fully functioning, social cat. Play and mock fighting, as well as shared-cleaning and similar, more gentle activities, have a deep-seated, much needed purpose in the life of the kitten. Cats deprived of such interaction often develop into antisocial and underdeveloped adults.

**Individual Personalities**

This is not to say that all kittens develop along the same path, in the same way, at the same rate. From the earliest displays of

*Each kitten develops at its own rate and within its own inherent personality. For some, exploration of the world beyond the nest becomes a priority much earlier than for others.*

*Kittens generally make their break with the litter and with their mother, and set out on their own at three to six months of age.*

*Although tree-climbing is something that most kittens eventually attempt and experience, some are naturally and instinctively more suited to the activity.*

*Some female cats are more protective of their kittens than others. This Abyssinian queen obviously is somewhat distressed over how exposed she and her kitten are for the photo.*

*The experiences of kittens with the litter-mates in their first few weeks of life are critical to their adult-hood, when they call on those early experiences for the basis of their reactions to various situations.*

*The 'meow' begins as the call of a kitten in need of something, but carries over in many into adulthood. It can signal a very wide range of emotions and conditions.*

*The first vocalisation for any cat is between kitten and mother. Purring is the perfect communication at this time in life because it can be accomplished without the interruption of other activities.*

*Kittens readily extend their play to include, in addition to their mother and littermates, a wide variety of objects. The ball of yarn has become a cliché in this respect.*

*For as long as she will permit it, the queen remains a target of her kittens' play. Within a few weeks she usually will begin to distance herself from her kittens' flurry of activity.*

*Any surface or level within reach of the kitten is fair game in its constant drive to encounter new experiences and explore new realms.*

*Early experiences help to mold the personality of a cat, preparing it for activities later in life. However, some kittens, like this Bengal jumping from rock to rock along the beach, are naturally more outgoing.*

*Whilst play with its mother can become very spirited and rambunctious, the kitten also spends a great deal of quiet, caring time with the queen.*

personality, every litter of kittens demonstrates the individuality of its members. Almost without variation, each litter will include a dominant member, one or more very submissive members, and a range of others falling between those extremes. There also will be variations in how outgoing the kittens will be, how they take to being handled by humans, and how much playfulness they carry with them into later life, as well as a spectrum of other personality characteristics.

The young cat will encounter a similar hierarchy amongst other cats as well when it begins to move out from the litter and into the wider world. Cats are much more social than many of us imagine. Often we keep them as individuals indoors, and by default the pet owner becomes the focus of their socialisation.

In contact with other cats, the kitten will be faced with carving a niche for itself. Older cats familiar with each other and each others' capabilities are already established in the neighbourhood hierarchy, so the newcomer generally must fight for a position in that chain of command. Even within a domicile that houses more than one cat, the felines will struggle to establish their positions and a kitten will eventually be forced into this fray.

### A Need for Society

The cat that finds no outlets for its social side—in other cats, other pets, or in humans—often will fall into antisocial behaviour patterns, which can include urinating in inappropriate locations, self-mutilation, clawing of furniture and chewing of carpeting, or incessant caterwauling.

In normally developed cats, the two most widely recognised vocalisations of cats arise

*Any space that can accommodate the paw of a kitten holds a natural attraction. There's no telling what wonderful plaything might be found in that hole and pulled out for closer inspection.*

*Well-socialised kittens are generally calmer, more comfortable with situations, and more open to encounters with the unknown and the unexpected.*

Interaction with their siblings is extremely important in preparing kittens to be social, non-neurotic cats later in life. Play is an integral part of that relationship.

Cats display many tendencies toward a somewhat social existence, although not to the extent that dogs do, who are by nature pack animals.

Some kittens find that climbing trees really is not for them. Unfortunately, they inevitably discover this after they have attempted the climb and gotten themselves stranded.

in kittenhood. 'Meow' is the call the kitten will give out when it is uncomfortable, unhappy, or uncertain. Everything from being lost to being disturbed from sleep can cause the kitten to react in this way. Variations on the meow carry over into adulthood, covering everything from confusion to sexual arousal.

Similarly, purring begins early in the life of a kitten. It is used first to communicate the young cat's contentment to its mother. Purring can be accomplished without interrupting nursing, so it is the perfect vocalisation for this purpose. The mother will return the purr to comfort her kittens. Later the kittens will purr to register their readiness for play and to signal their submission to a more dominant playmate or aggressor. Purring remains throughout the lives of most cats, employed for various reasons.

*Following page: A high vantage point is welcomed by many kittens when they reach the age at which they begin to explore their world more avidly.*

*The kitten deprived of normal social development may very likely develop antisocial behaviours, including an aversion to being held and a tendency toward a 'loner' lifestyle.*

*As the young cat moves out beyond the confines of the nest and the protection of its mother, it will encounter the territories of other cats who may or may not be receptive to its crossing of the 'fence'— whether a physical fence or some instinctive barrier.*

*Within every litter of kittens the individual members display distinct personalities. Dominant characteristics, outgoing tendencies, and the like are displayed very early in the kittens' lives.*

*In a great many cats the fear of dogs is a learnt behaviour. As such, an affinity for dogs can be introduced into a kitten's personality through early, non-threatening, comfortable exposure.*

# THE ELEMENTS OF PLAY

In the first few days of a kitten's life there is little activity other than eating, sleeping, and snuggling with mother. The kitten's eyes won't open fully until one to three weeks after birth. The queen may decide to move her litter within this period, sometimes repeatedly, responding to an instinctive urge to find better protection for them.

The kittens, however, won't begin to crawl about to any great extent until their second week; walking will occur at about three weeks, and running at four or five weeks. Also at four or five weeks, the kitten will begin to make attempts to clean itself by licking.

### Breakdown of the Bond

At this point the bond between queen and kitten begins to weaken. Although the mother still makes herself available enough for nursing to provide adequate nourishment to the kittens, they are now able to handle some solid food and suckling oppor-

*Kittens denied exposure to siblings within the first eight weeks of their lives often carry strange and undesirable behaviours and habits into adulthood.*

*Kittens, when not sleeping, are always ready for play. An impish playfulness shines through the eyes of this gray Persian. Whatever opportunity presents itself, she appears ready to take part.*

*A great deal of the motions used in sibling play are actually precursors to hunting activity later in the life. Kittens have an instinctive inclination in this regard.*

tunities begin to grow noticeably fewer. The queen also grows less accepting of play directed at her by the kittens. She will move away from annoying members of the litter, and sometimes cuff them a bit. Often she will be seen sitting at some distance, but still well within range of immediate protection if necessary.

This distancing will become more pronounced as the kittens become more mobile. Within days the queen will find it an impossible task to keep all the kittens together at all times. If possible she will now position herself on some elevated location nearby. From there she will oversee the activities of her brood, occasionally jumping down to retrieve the boldest of the kittens who range too far despite her calls from the perch.

The bond may weaken, but if the queen and her kittens remain in contact on something close to a daily basis, she may very well hold onto some of her motherly feelings well into the kittens' adulthood. This relationship may even see a mother offering food to her grown children.

*The period from the third or fourth week of a kitten's life through the eighth week is one of huge development and a refinement of skills and abilities.*

*Tag is a favourite game amongst kittens. However, determining exactly who is 'it' is nearly impossible for all but those involved in the game.*

The bond with the mother begins to weaken around the fifth week of life and kittens will move off on their own for individual explorations by the eighth week.

This kitten is signaling a readiness for some rough, fast play with nearly every fibre of its being, from its bright eyes to its erect ears to its alert tail.

For developing kittens it seems there is always something more interesting on the other side. Every barrier must be conquered.

### First Priority: Play

On the other hand, this is the time that play activities get under way in earnest for her offspring, with hunting-oriented practise coming in the six- to eight-week range. Now the kitten will undergo incredibly fast development; the arrival of a fully independent being by the age of six months is common.

There is always plenty of time for play in a kitten's life. Wrestling, tackling, and tagging one another and other objects—both living and inanimate—fill their days.

At times their attacks on one another may seem quite fierce and potentially injurious, but generally it's all just a game and no one receives lasting harm. If one notes the exaggerated movements and attitudes displayed by the playing kittens, the element of fun is apparent.

Play for the kittens can include any or all of the following: chasing one's own tail, pouncing on some imagined object, rearing onto one's hind legs to encourage an attack from a littermate, wrestling matches with the aggressor and defender roles switching back and forth quickly and unpredictably, snatching at one another's paws, and biting at one another's neck. Any number of the kittens in a litter may be involved in playing at any given moment. A common ending to the

*Hanging objects hold a particular fascination for kittens because of the constant motion, with just the slightest paw-slash, they can bring to the play session.*

*A ball of yarn makes for a fine prey specimen in the eyes of a housebound kitten. All the motions of the hunt can be practised on that ball of yarn and, as it roles or bounces away, it almost takes on a life of its own.*

*No possible source of play is overlooked by kittens. The dark, unknown inside of this vase is a 'must-see' for this American shorthair.*

*Hunting is an instinctive behaviour in nearly all cats, but each kitten must learn successful techniques in order to fulfill its natural role as hunter and killer.*

play period is the chasing about, in no particular or planned fashion, of all of the participants.

This flurry of activity is a way for kittens to discover, develop, and refine their abilities and skills for use in later life. Kittens denied this early play often appear underdeveloped as adults. For instance, whilst an attacker is developing his or her offensive skills, the attacked at the same time is developing the skills of defence. Later the roles, and the learning, will be reversed. A kitten engineering an attack on a ball of yarn is actually putting itself through all the phases of the hunt—stalking, ambushing, pouncing, pinning, biting, and killing.

## Becoming the Hunter

Although hunting is an instinctive behaviour in nearly all kittens, young cats need to learn to hunt successfully—that is, hunting *and* making the kill—by observing their mothers. If the queen is an experienced and successful hunter who is allowed to hunt and kill, the kittens generally will follow in that lineage.

At about three weeks the queen will begin to bring killed prey back to the kittens and

*Climbing is a favourite exploratory method for kittens. Even the thinnest of branches is attractive to them.*

eat it whilst they watch. In another week or two, when the kittens are ready to begin eating solids, she will start to share the prey with the kittens. After another few weeks she will offer live prey to the kittens, allowing them to make the kill themselves. The final lessons come when the kittens begin to follow their mother on her hunts, and eventually when they make a kill completely on their own.

Although several kittens will attack the prey brought back by their mother, sometimes in tandem, they actually are developing individual hunting skills. With few exceptions cats are not pack hunters. They generally are better adapted to ambush and stalking styles of hunting, rather than running down their prey. In the wild there are some notable exceptions, such as the lion, which relies on numbers to bring down large prey for the group, and the cheetah, which relies on its incredible speed to outrun its prey. But domestic cats almost always are oriented to loner status when it comes to hunting.

*Following page: Of course, one never knows when the latest climbing expedition will come to a dead end, either real or imagined. Then it's time to get a good claw-hold and figure out the next move.*

*Plants and the soil in which they grow are always of interest to exploring kittens. They have a whole range of activities that can involve plants, which includes digging, nibbling, and scratching.*

*Kittens do not begin to get around very well until their third to fifth week of life. But from that point forward, it's anyone's guess as to where they might turn up and what they might do.*

## Human Contact

During the development period in the kittens' lives, contact with humans can be an important supplement to their mother's care. Although nothing can replace a kitten's mother (cats that have grown up without maternal direction tend to be shy and easily frightened throughout adulthood), young cats that receive human handling generally develop more quickly in all areas. Their eyes open earlier, their senses and abilities are demonstrated earlier, and there may even be some evidence that patterns in their fur appear earlier. Apparently the addi-

*Many kittens have a slightly standoffish attitude toward being handled by humans. They must be approached slowly, quietly, and gently to help them overcome such concerns.*

*Kittens allowed to roam outdoors will include a much larger range within their daily rounds, and with it a wider set of experiences. However, that same extension can bring them into contact with many additional dangers.*

tional handling stimulates those areas of the brain and nervous system in kittens that control development.

Such early handling, of course, also assists in the development of a human-friendly cat that usually won't object to handling later in life. Unfortunately, for some kittens, the bond with humans can become overly strong. These animals can actually get too dependent upon human contact; they may even focus all of their need on an individual human and carry it throughout their lives. Such cats tend to overreact, even to the point of becoming physically ill, when left to themselves for even brief periods of time. Their poor reactions may also include a deterioration in learnt behaviour, such as in the use of its litter pan.

*A kitten's involvement with a ball of yarn can become very intense indeed. Such activity should be encouraged in order to build a more well-balanced, socialised, active cat later in life.*

*The sense of constant curiosity evident in kittens is a natural wonder worth long and careful observation.*

# KITTEN SELECTION AND CARE

Most of us want to begin our association with a cat at its youngest age possible, so as not to miss any of the cute-and-cuddly stage. For the safety and health of the kitten, this generally means about six- to eight-weeks old. Kittens are generally not fully weaned from their mother until about their eighth week. (They continue, however, to need milk as part of their daily diet until approximately six months of age.)

Whilst the kitten has a great deal of appeal, there are those instances in which a new owner may want to opt for an adult cat. If the cat is to be left alone for lengthy periods of time from the start, an adult cat generally requires less supervision and would be the better choice for a new cat owner. Kittens, after all, need frequent feedings throughout the day and their litter-box etiquette is of course still being

*Selecting just the right kitten from a whole mass of little balls of fur can be both an enjoyable and a confusing moment. Will the kitten carry those traits through to adulthood?*

*The Japanese bobtail is an ancient breed in its native Japan, where the calico variety is considered extremely lucky; the namesake bobtail doesn't show on these kittens.*

developed. Additionally, with an adult cat, a prospective owner can get a more thorough preview of personality traits and quirks of the new housemate. Of course this also means the pet owner will have very little impact on the development of these traits. A final factor to consider in the adult-cat-or-kitten question is the fact that kittens have a lot of energy that must by nature be played out, and this will require some time and patience as it gets accustomed to its new home.

Today, because kittens primarily come from pet shops and because families are encouraged by those concerned with overpopulation to have their animals spayed or neutered, very few people get the opportunity to actually witness the birth of kittens, or even to see newborns. By all means, if you know someone, a breeder perhaps, whose queen is pregnant or recently gave birth to kittens, take the opportunity to view them. Depending on breed and heritage their appearance will vary, but for the most part, they will be small, quiet, helpless, and generally irresistible.

## Pedigree or Mixed Breed

It may seem at first to be a simple choice between choosing a pedigree or a non-pedigree cat. If you want to show and/or breed the cat, the pedigree is of course essential. In addition, a purebred cat will display certain inherited traits and characteristics, so you can be fairly certain as to how it will look and what its temperament might be when it's grown.

There are more than one hundred breeds of cats in the world. Unlike dogs, which vary greatly in size and shape, domestic cats vary little in regard to the size of their bodies.

Also unlike dogs, cats are not categorised into groups like sporting dogs, hounds, working dogs, terriers, toy dogs, and herding dogs. Longhairs and shorthairs more or less covers cat categorisation.

However, this does not mean that some breeds are not generally acknowledged as having a specific personality trait. Your local cat club or any number of good reference books can inform you of the various traits of certain breeds. For example, the Siamese cat is generally known as an outgoing,

*Although pedigree breeds receive a great deal of attention, for the vast majority of cat owners, the non-pedigree is the natural choice, based more on the personality evidenced by the individual kitten.*

*When introducing a kitten to its new home, it's best to give it as much latitude and exploration time on its own as possible. Of course, it still needs to be under observation to protect it from any unsuspected dangers.*

affectionate breed, which responds to attention from its owner and displays a strong loyalty. Similarly, the White Persian is prized by those in search of affectionate, but calm and restrained cats.

Naturally, you can expect to pay handsomely for the pedigree; thus if your goals are as explained above, or if you simply must have a particular breed, you leave yourself little choice.

If a non-pedigree is more your style, however, be prepared for a kitten that may or may not grow into the cat you thought it would. The previous owner may explain that it is a mix of certain breeds, but if no one knows its heritage for sure, you may find out differently as the kitten grows.

There are many nuances within both the pedigree and the non-pedigree question, as well as between the two options. Notably, there are the pet-quality pedigree cats. These are animals that result from a mating of pedigree lines but don't exhibit all the standard configurations and patterns required for show competition.

Then there are the choices amongst the various pedigree breeds, ranging from the small, so-called hairless Sphynx to the large Maine coon longhair. Personal preference plays a part here, but so should care requirements. Longhair breeds, like the Persians, for example, need almost daily grooming. In addition to the obvious physical variations, personality traits have been ascribed to many of the breeds in existence today. Of course when dealing with individual animals, *every* rule can be potentially broken.

Millions of cat owners—the vast majority, in fact—never even consider a choice amongst breeds. They want a companion cat with whom they can share their homes and lives, and the first kitten whose charms prove irresistible will be selected.

For these people the local animal shelter generally provides a wide selection of kittens, all of which are in dire need of a home. This, by the way, is also the choice that most benefits an overcrowded world, filled each day with new litters of unwanted kittens.

## Finding a Healthy Kitten

When selecting a kitten for which you have no show or breeding expectations, it is considered best to pick the individual that appears both larger and bolder than the others housed with it. This kitten probably is demonstrating its fine health and physical abilities. In addition, if an individual comes forward, you have some indication of a

*The more outgoing kittens generally will exhibit and demonstrate this characteristic when they encounter new situations, such as when someone is looking them over to choose which one will have a new home.*

*Raising onto the hind legs is generally a kitten's plea for activity and play. Usually it is directed toward other kittens.*

bright and clear? Is the nose moist? Are the teeth white? Is the tongue pink? Are the ears dry and clean?

The sex of the kitten is usually the next consideration. If you are going to the do the right thing and, with all cats not intended for show or breeding, castrate all toms and spay all queens to prevent unwanted litters, the sex choice is one you really don't need to make. There is very little difference between a castrated tom and a spayed queen.

By contrast, the non-castrated tom will spray furniture with urine, roam far beyond the home on a regular basis, and engage in numerous fights with other toms; the non-spayed queen will enter periods of heat throughout the year, with a number of unpleasant personality changes, and always carries the risk of unwanted pregnancy.

Determining the sex of a young kitten can be a confusing task and, unless you are experienced at it, you may want to consult an expert for an examination of the anal area of the cat. A female kitten's vulva will be very close to her anus, even to the point that it may appear the two openings are actually joined. A male kitten will have a raised, dark area beneath the anus. This will eventually develop into larger testicles, with the cat's penis lying beneath it.

*Most new cat owners prefer to begin their association with a very young kitten, but they must be aware that the younger cat will require more care and attention and may get into additional 'situations'.*

friendly and playful temperament, if such is your requirement.

However, there are a few more checks on its overall health that should be run on any kitten before the final decision is made. Here are a few questions to ask yourself during hands-on inspection of the animal: Does the animal walk with a limp or any other abnormality? Is the anal area clean? Is the coat smooth, or are there mats in it? Is there any evidence of fleas or ticks? Are the eyes

*Kittens should remain with their mother until at least six weeks, or better yet eight weeks, of age. Earlier removal from the queen often results in underdeveloped, dysfunctional cats.*

The new kitten, with big eyes filled with wonderment, instills in us a deep sense of wonder as well. However, only through a great deal of patience and effort will an owner and cat arrive at the ideal relationship.

Although there is less variation between cat breeds than there is between dog breeds, there is still a great deal of choice available in the Cat Fancy. One of the rarer breeds is the Devon rex.

## The New Home

With the new member of the family selected you're ready to take the kitten home. A crate is the safest way to transport any small animal in a vehicle. The urge to hold the new kitten in your lap will be understandably strong, but it is best for everyone if the kitten is enclosed safely for the trip.

Is your home ready for the introduction? There are many dangers in the average home for an unsuspecting cat.

Plants hold a particular attraction for most cats, who react in a range of ways, from outright attack to a gentle nibbling.

Unfortunately many common houseplants are quite poisonous to cats. Some to be aware of are azalea, caladiums, dieffenbachia, hyacinth, laurel, lily-of-the-valley, lobelia, mistletoe, narcissus, oleander, and primrose. Persistent plant-loving cats can be deterred with odorless, cat-repellent sprays and by giving them their own box-gardens of planted herbs or grasses.

Other dangers around the home include exposed electrical cords that can be chewed, sharp utensils, toxic household cleansers and similar products, open appliance doors, plastic bags, small objects that can be swallowed,

*Following page: Persians have a reputation as affectionate, calm, and easygoing— the perfect indoor cat for a relatively quiet, infant-free, comfortable household.*

*In its new home the kitten will encounter many new objects and experiences, some of which can be harmful to the unsuspecting animal. It is the owner's responsibility to police the home before bringing the kitten there.*

*Crates made for carrying cats in cars make ideal beds in the home, because they can be latched and can provide a very secure feeling for the animal.*

household trash and garbage cans, and open fireplaces.

After the dangers have been dealt with, it's time to let your kitten explore its new home. Don't immediately overwhelm it with too many people. Take a few minutes first to show the kitten its sleeping area, and give it time to examine everything in peace. Don't alarm it with loud noises; talk softly to it and pet it. It will soon come to understand that this is its new home. Finally, gradually introduce the kitten to other members of the family.

## Safe and Secure

The kitten's bed should be in a draft-free area that is out of the lane of traffic. Because it may have accidents, a non-carpeted area is preferred, as is one that can be closed off from the rest of the house. The bed can be a wooden box, a basket, or a box lined with a rug or blanket.

Crates made for carrying cats in cars also make ideal bed areas because they can be latched, and within it the animal may feel very secure. The kitten should be shown its food and water dishes, and given its first meal in its new home as soon as possible. For this introductory meal, give it about a third less than is normal, and keep a distance whilst it eats.

Now allow the kitten to roam about and investigate all areas of the house that it will

*For showing or breeding, a pedigree cat is absolutely essential. This playful little one is a pure-bred Tonkinese.*

*Before the age of six to eight weeks, the kitten, both physically and mentally, is not ready to leave its mother.*

*No matter how interesting their environment and playmates, a big part of kittens' lives is spent asleep. They make up for all that rest of course with a great deal of activity whilst awake.*

*Within even the pedigree breeds there is wide variation, and many purebred cats come up short on the standard lines and markings agreed upon by governing organisations. These are often referred to as pet-quality cats.*

be permitted to occupy, with no interference from other pets and little from humans. It will eventually settle down after it has satisfied its curiosity.

If you've waited until the kitten's eighth week or so to bring it home, you won't need to concern yourself with the weaning process. You can begin giving the kitten solid, minced foods right away. Two or three meals a day and a saucer of milk somewhere in between will be all the kitten needs to thrive. Rely on a commercial, nutritionally balanced food.

### Litter-box Training
Luckily for us, cats are naturally very clean animals; most actually prefer to bury their feces. Hence, the litter box offers a natural attraction for the kitten when nature calls.

Locate the litter box or pan in some convenient place for the kitten, but one where he or she will feel calm and secure. Place the young cat in the pan frequently, particularly when it shows signs of needing to defecate or urinate (such as crouching with its tail raised).

Problems in accepting the litter pan are generally due to its having a location where the cat feels disturbed or intruded upon, a fragrance in the litter that the cat doesn't like, or litter that is not cleaned frequently enough.

*Although new kittens should be watched with care, we should remember that exploring, even high above the ground, is important to their development.*

*'Go ahead. Just try and resist me', this kitten seems to be saying to a passerby outside its home.*

When a kitten does relieve itself in the wrong location, rubbing its nose in it will *not* serve the purpose you intend. That will only convince the kitten that the spot it chose is indeed the toilet because of the scent it now more firmly associates there. Instead, carry the kitten to the litter pan immediately. Better yet, try to catch the kitten just as it is ready to defecate or urinate and then carry it to the litter pan.

The key at all times in training a kitten—or an adult cat for that matter—is patience, reward, and praise, along with a complete absence of physical punishment and scolding. Probably no single sentence in this book is more valuable in the development of your relationship with your kitten.

*Some breeds are associated with certain characteristics. For example, these Maine coon kittens most likely will be hearty cats with even dispositions and a love for the outdoors.*

*Patience, a gentle touch, calm tones, reward, and praise are critical in developing a warm and affectionate long-term relationship with a kitten.*

# INDEX

*Page numbers in **bold-face** type indicate photo captions.*